FOOD FROM THE KITCHEN GARDEN

A Kitchen Garden Book

By the same Author.
In the same series:
Keeping a Few Hens in your Garden
Beekeeping for Beginners (with Penelope Hands)
Keeping a Few Ducks in your Garden
A Peacock on the Lawn (with S. Carpenter)
Goose on the Green
Also:
The Big Book of Garden Hens
A Henkeeper's Journal
A Christmas Journal

Published by the Kitchen Garden 1998
Church Lane, Troston
Bury St Edmunds Suffolk IP31 1EX
Tel 01359 268 322
Email: francine@jfraymond.demon.co.uk
www.kitchen-garden-hens.co.uk

ISBN 0-9532857-0-7

Printed in England on recycled paper

Many thanks to: Barbara Hurn, Carla Carlisle, Joy Larkom
Jo Kendall and Leslie Forbes.

1

'For what was Paradise, but a garden?
An orchard of trees and herbs.
Full of pleasure and nothing there but delights.'
William Lawson 1618

Introduction

One of my greatest pleasures is to watch the seasons change in my garden, through the window and on my plate. A greedy eater, passionate gardener and hen keeper, I like to eat food grown and raised myself, or at least to try and buy what's in season: to create some kind of intimacy with the source of my ingredients and to claim the joy of growing, picking and eating.

I have a small country garden with a vegetable patch where produce is grown naturally with the help and hindrance of a few hens. I also run a pocket-sized shop where stock reflects these passions. The dishes in this book are those I cook for myself, family and friends, as well as customers who make their way to the Kitchen Garden. The ingredients come mostly from my own plot: vegetables, herbs, salads, fruit, nuts and eggs, but I'm by no means self-sufficient, in fact I'm pretty familiar with the shelves at my local supermarket. I think that good cooking is more than recipes, more inspiration than instruction, and this collection is really a flexible medley of ingredients for you to alter to suit your tastes, appetite and harvest.

Above all, this is real cooking, not as performed on television - I am fairly unobtrusive, have a horror of motorbikes and sidecars and rarely dance in the kitchen. My meals are cooked everyday to no rapturous applause and often without the approval of my offspring who dream of takeaway pizzas. Still I feel that the pleasure of the freshest fruit and vegetables, the deep yellow yolks of a favourite hen's eggs, the fragrance of herbs and above all the taste of what grows in your own garden is as close to Paradise as we get.

ANUARY- Celeriac

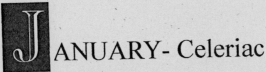

I never noticed Winter when I lived in town. Here on the grain prairies of Suffolk though, January gets into your bones. Time spent in the garden is kept to a shivery minimum. I grab what I need from the vegetable plot and scuttle inside. Better to watch what's going on through the kitchen window.

A glimpse of the hens is a tonic. Intrepid, they strut and flutter providing the drama and colour that's missing from most gardens at this time of the year. Time to take stock, keep warm and eat. One of my favourite winter dishes is a sort of mixed vegetable mash. Pure comfort food, it even co-stars with the goose on our Christmas menu.

I extricate from the mud as many root vegetables as I can find: celeriacs like boulders and giant parsnips are a must, and carrots, and jerusalem artichokes. Also a few leeks. I cherish my beautiful blue/green leeks (var. Blue Wila or St Victor). I always have at least four rows at different stages of growth and leave a few to flower.

For the mash: fry the finely chopped leeks with a pinch of cumin in some goose fat or butter, adding all the peeled chopped roots and turn till sealed. Ladle in a little stock or water to stop the contents sticking, then cover and turn down the heat. When the celeriac is tender, mash with crème fraîche and season. Sprinkle

some chopped flat-leaved parsley on top and serve. **This purée could be diluted more and put in the blender to make a good thick soup.**

I grow celeriac (var: Snow White) from seed in pots in the greenhouse and plant out in May. It likes a damp spot, not exactly plentiful here. I try to remember to water. Celeriac has always been more popular in Germany than this country, so this is a recipe given by my friend Monika from Heidelberg. **Boil the peeled, chopped celeriac in salty water with two tablespoons of white wine vinegar to stop discolouring. When soft, strain, and slice finely, using the reduced liquor to make a dressing with oil, chopped shallots, parsley and a few green celeriac leaves. Season well.** The vinaigrette will go deliciously gelatinous and will keep for a week in the fridge.

EBRUARY- Brassicas

Ignored and unvisited during its wintry quarantine, my kitchen garden looks almost tropical. Crinkly blue/green Savoys, elegantly ribbed purple January Kings and multicoloured kales and sprouts, started in pots in the Spring and Autumn, now look as luscious as a tapestry by Klimt, especially when frosted with their outer leaves nibbled to lace by the hens. The huge range of brassicas offers a wide spectrum of winter greenery. The key to this cornucopia is Joy Larkom's book 'Creative Vegetable Gardening'.

Although I can muster little enthusiasm for cooked cabbage *per se*, there are several dishes I crave after the rich largesse of Christmas. Cavolo Nero or Tuscan Kale is a stunning dark green palm tree of a brassica. In Summer I underplant it with orange pot marigolds and the top leaves can be harvested throughout the year for *minestras* and stir-fries. **Try it ribboned with a little pancetta or sundried tomato and pine nuts. Stir fry briefly till floppy but still crunchy. Add a few drops of tamari sauce and sesame oil and serve.**

Red cabbage is an exotic looking plant that livens up garden and plate. **In a heavy lidded pan, I fry a couple of red onions and green apples in a little olive oil with a tablespoon of light muscovado sugar. From the mortar and pestle I add crushed garlic, sea salt, juniper berries, and coloured peppercorns, sprinkled with ground allspice and a clove or two, and then I put**

in the finely sliced red cabbage. Cook for 15 minutes with a splash of balsamic vinegar.

I have a lovely black French lidded cast-iron pan bought from the Elizabeth David shop. It cost more than three times what I paid for my first car - £30, but it caters for a family of four all through the year.

These hearty dishes along with the occasional bursts of pale February sunshine fill me with energy. I want to get out and dig. The hens would love it: a few tasty worms and leatherjackets, but chilblains and experience tell me that an untidy garden offers frost protection till Spring. I'll sit down and get out the gardening books and magazines instead.

ARCH - Eggs

Everything in the garden has been given the green light to go. All my hens are laying, except the broody Nell, who seems to have retired. Still frenetically maternal, she looks after all her past offspring, clucking and offering food to elderly daughters who can't believe their luck. She will sit on anything and I am going to get her to hatch some Buff Orpington eggs to replace my beloved Babe, who died last year.

There's masses to do in the garden and to get the shop ready by May, so I need fast food. I've picked a colander of new spinach from the cloche plus a few early sorrel leaves. Nestled among the tender plants is a freshly laid egg, a gift for my lunch.

Rinsing the leaves carefully to remove the grit splashed up from the recent showers - gritty spinach is not pleasant, I put them in my black pan with a knob of butter and a pinch of sea-salt. A minute later the spinach has almost disappeared and must be drained, chopped and drained again.

Meanwhile, I boil some water in a kettle and pour it into a frying pan. As soon as the water starts to bubble, I crack the fresh egg in very carefully for one minute, and removing the pan from the heat, leave it and the egg to stand till cooked. They say eggs should be cooked right through the yolk. I prefer mine runny, but it's a small risk for those who know the egg's provenance.

Removing the poached egg from the water with a slotted spoon, I pop it on the mound of spinach, and grate a little parmesan, nutmeg, and black pepper. If you need something a little more sustaining, place the whole concoction on a slice of. grilled polenta.

Another lunch dish that relies on really fresh eggs is *oeuf en cocotte*. Fry some chopped leeks and place in the bottom of a well buttered ramekin dish. Bury a little nugget of pecorino or parmesan among the leeks and crack an egg on top. Cover with crème fraîche, sprinkle with nutmeg and place the dish in a covered pan of boiling shallow water until the egg is cooked to your liking. Serve this with toast soldiers.

If eggs were rarer, they would be keenly sought after and as greatly appreciated as truffles.

OTHER things to do with Eggs.

If you keep hens, now is a time of surfeit. Reward them well, they are working hard. For a special treat give them some sunflower seed hearts. Here are a few ideas to make use of the extra bounty.

To make homemade marzipan for an Easter Simnel cake: **take equal amounts of sugar and ground almonds, and bind them together with beaten egg and a squeeze of lemon juice. Mix, then knead and roll out, using sprinkled icing sugar to stop the paste sticking to your board. Place a thick layer of marzipan on top of your fruit cake, plus eleven small balls as decoration. The whole cake can be popped under the grill to brown.** Any leftover marzipan can be moulded into small Easter eggs and dipped in melted chocolate.

Clafoutis **is a Mediterranean pancake dish of seasonal fruit with a vanilla flavoured 4 egg batter poured over it. Then it's baked in the oven till brown and sprinkled with caster sugar. At this time of the year you could use rhubarb, but later in the season, why not try gooseberries, cherries or my favourite - apricots.** You can make a delicious savoury pancake by adding a purée of any cooked vegetable to a basic batter. Baked mashed aubergine with basil, or fried courgettes with rosemary are tasty, but chopped spinach or chard are good too.

Nougat is one of life's true delicacies. **Heat half a pound of sugar with a little water and orange flower essence to hard ball consistency when dropped into a saucer of water. At the same time heat a pan of the same amount of honey - this time to the soft ball stage and combine the two. An extra pair of hands is useful. Fold in 4 beaten egg whites. Return this *mélange* to the stove, stirring constantly for what seems like forever (in fact half an hour) until the mixture is thick and white. Then add halved hazelnuts and bits of chopped orange zest and pour the nougat into an oiled pan lined with rice paper and leave to cool.** Cut into small rectangular pieces. Wrapped prettily, it makes a lovely Easter present - if you haven't eaten the whole lot in a self congratulationary binge.

APRIL - Rhubarb

For months the fruit bowl has been dominated by apples, oranges and bananas, so the sight of early pink rhubarb shoots is as welcome as the first fritillaries. The plants have escaped the frosts cocooned in straw and topped with a bamboo cloche to stop the hens eating the leaves. It just shows what iron constitutions chickens have to survive such a massive dose of oxalic acid.

An article by Sophie Grigson first alerted me to the joys of cooking angelica and rhubarb together. So as a change from the usual partnership of ginger and orange, **I cut both into inch sized chunks (at a ratio of 3/1 rhubarb to angelica) and cook for 7 minutes on a very low heat with light muscovado sugar and a knob of butter.** Forced rhubarb needs less sweetening.

I add a few chopped angelica leaves to the custard I eat with my compote. Homemade custard, like mayonnaise is a far cry from the shop bought variety. After years of curdled custard, I now add a teaspoon of cornflour to the cooking. **I heat a pint of single cream or milk plus the angelica leaves to boiling point and very slowly add it to a bowl containing three beaten egg yolks, a tablespoon of sugar and the cornflour. Stirring constantly, I strain the mixture and return the whole lot to the heat, and carry on stirring till the custard thickens.** Cooled and combined with any fruit purée, this mixture can be frozen to make icecream. I have a useful and inexpensive *gelatiera* that sits in the freezer ready for use. My sons have invented some truly disgusting icecream flavours, tomato ketchup features heavily.

Both rhubarb (var: Cawood Delight has beautiful red stems) and angelica with its massive seed heads - and millions of seedlings, are handsome architectural plants that are easy to grow and add height and structure to any ornamental kitchen garden. Bronze fennel, a pest because it also pops up everywhere, artichokes (see August) and cardoons all give the vegetable plot a sense of scale.

AY - Elderflowers

The shop and garden are open, and customers who drive a long way deserve something delicious to eat with their coffee or tisane. My friend Barbara is justly renowned for her cakes and also makes a fragrant elderflower cordial which decanted into pretty bottles, sells out as soon as the year's vintage hits the shelves. I hoard a supply for muscat flavoured gooseberry fools and icecreams and also for this wonderfully easy and now famous Elderflower, Lemon and Sweet Cicely Sponge.

Barbara bakes a light single decker sponge with lots of fresh eggs. While the cake is still warm from the oven I grate lemon zest on top, and drizzle liberal amounts of elderflower cordial over the surface so that it literally becomes a sponge and soaks up the sweet liquid. Decorated with sweet cicely leaves, doillied and sitting on a glass plate, each gooey slice is dredged with icing sugar. This cake has turned customers into constant friends.

Once used to flavour Chartreuse, I grow sweet cicely in the wild garden. It seeds itself everywhere and the delicate ferns can be added to tart fruits like rhubarb and gooseberries as a pleasant way to reduce their acid bite. I have grown Elders as standard trees in the garden and they look pretty away from the roadside hedgerows and consequent lead contamination.

To make the cordial, pick 10 creamy flowerheads on a sunny day. Soak them in 1½ pints boiled cooled water in a large pan or clean bucket containing 1¾ lbs of sugar (light muscovado makes a stronger tasting, darker liquid) 1 oz tartaric acid (from the chemist) and a whole sliced lemon. All the ingredients should be stirred periodically over 24 hours and then strained through a muslin lined sieve. Finally decant and once opened, keep cold - if you can keep it at all.

We are all raising a glass of cordial to the health of Nellie's two new Buff Orpington babies - mother and chicks are doing well.

JUNE - Asparagus

It's Midsummer day and although I feel we've barely started, it's already time to stop picking the asparagus. I know other crops will take its place, but there's nothing quite like your own asparagus, grown in a raised bed with plenty of grit to open up the soil.

This green soup copes with the sporadic yield you get at the beginning and end of the season: with rude spears that are too big and tough or sprue that's too small and weedy. It has nettle tops as its base, plus small amounts of early Summer vegetables.

I finely chop and fry a few leeks in butter, with a couple of potatoes and a bag full of nettle tops that I've tentatively collected wearing gloves, under my neighbour's quizzical stare. Trimmed from their stalks with scissors, I add to the nettles a few asparagus spears or stalks, some salad burnet, garlic chives, flat-leaved parsley and anything else that's green and non cabbagelike.

Sweated and diluted with stock, as soon as the potatoes are soft, I season and put the lot into the blender and then re-heat with a little lemon juice and crème fraîche for a surprisingly delicate, nourishing late Spring tonic.

17

In full season I eat asparagus whenever I can, steamed, grilled or raw, but my favourite lunch consists of a few choice spears, boiled with the tough base stem left on, so that they can be easily picked up and dipped into soft boiled eggs, with a piece of homemade bread, a few shavings of parmesan cheese and eaten in the sun in the garden with the hens as my companions, hoping for the crumbs.

Jane Grigson liked to cook a few new potatoes with her asparagus. This is the perfect marriage. The asparagus benefit from the support the potatoes give and they in return are improved by the flavour of the asparagus water. It's a bit like the relationship between hens and the vegetable garden; they eat the trimmings and leftovers and the beds are liberally manured and cleaned in the autumn - but we get the bonus - the eggs.

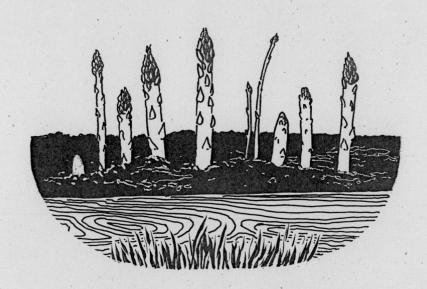

JULY - Salads

The kitchen table is moved outside onto the terrace in July, and we eat all our meals in the garden. I am reading Tom Jaine's book 'Building a Wood-Fired Oven' so we could cook outside without all the horrors of the barbecue. I love bricklaying, but this is major building work and I'll need help. Meanwhile there are so many good things to eat that don't need to be cooked.

Everyday before lunch I go out with scissors and bowl in hand to snip a variety of summer leaves. I wish my repertoire was as wide as John Evelyn's whose potager at Sayes Court was organized to produce salad throughout the year. I try to concoct a palette of colours, flavours and textures from red, through pink to all shades of green; from fernlike dill to crisp pak choi; from lemony buckler-leaved sorrel to the bitter chicories. Each day's salad is different, each meal is delicious. Often, because I don't spray my produce, the leaves do not need washing, just a dressing of good olive oil and vinegar.

To deter unwelcome diners, I keep low netted cages over my salad beds. In Winter they can be covered with fleece. I don't space the seeds, or transplant the seedlings, just snip off what I need. This stops the salads bolting and those that do, are given straight to the hens. There are more beaks to feed, Nell's chicks are already bigger than she is.

I augment my selection of leaves with handfuls of rocket, basil, coriander, mint, parsley or garlic chives from the herb garden; with young chard leaves, asparagus tips, baby leeks, and blanched runner beans from the vegetable plot - and in times of paucity with packs of saladini from the supermarket.

For pudding I eat strawberries topped with a few coriander flowers and leaves, and enhanced with tiny red or white Alpine berries (Fragaria semperflorens vesca). I love these neat little strawberry plants, their flavour is magical and they don't wander about the garden on runners like most wild varieties. Or I might pick a few red, white and black currants (which I grow as standards) sweetened with rose geranium flavoured sugar. Any surplus fruit is turned into sorbets, icecreams or coulis as a surprise later in the year or when all endeavour is beyond me, passed to Barbara to make her famous jams.

UGUST - Artichokes

Artichokes are my joy, my *plat de maison* and my trademark. I plant them everywhere: in the kitchen garden and in the borders. The most elegant and subtle of vegetables, their statuesque leaves and electric blue bee-studded chokes when left to flower are outstanding, to pick or leave to dry. I overwinter my plants (var: Vert de Laon) with a little straw under Thai bamboo cloches intended to house chickens but also useful to keep hens, cats, pigeons and the frost away from newly planted treasures. Artichokes grow well in an open soil, and should be divided in March so you never run short of plants.

My favourite way to eat artichokes is simply to boil them in salted water till the base of the stem is tender. Then we sit *en famille* with a huge plate of artichokes and a platter for the debris. We pick off the leaves one by one, dip them into a vinaigrette, pulling off the flesh with our teeth. When we get to the middle of the flower, we discard the fluffy choke, and mash the prized heart with dressing and scoff the lot. Heaven.

The refined way is to remove the tough outer layers before cooking, slice off the stalk and top third of the leaves, snipping off the leaf spikes and scooping out the hairy bits. Rub lemon juice over the cut surfaces and cook as before. You can then serve with a herby mayonnaise and hardboiled eggs to be mashed with the heart.

Homemade mayonnaise is wonderful. It uses an extravagant amount of oil (12 fluid oz to 3 eggs) and in August I can't even balance this with the thought of free eggs. All my ladies are moulting and off lay. **Bring all your ingredients out of the fridge or larder to room temperature. Take a very clean bowl, three egg yolks, a pinch of salt and whisk. Add a few drops of olive oil. Carry on whisking and adding small drips till the mixture thickens. Now you can add the rest of the oil in a steady stream. Finish with a squeeze of lemon juice. If your mayo curdles, just add another egg yolk and whisk again. Chopped chervil and tarragon are good additions, as is dill or a dash of Dijon mustard.**

August is my least favourite month. My greatest loves have flowered. It is bone dry. I close my shop and my eyes.

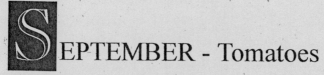EPTEMBER - Tomatoes

This is my favourite time of the year. The plants gain courage for a second flowering and in this light every flower counts. It is a time for picking, collecting and pillaging. In new feathered outfits, the hens are laying again, in secret places. When I get greedy and clear their nests of eggs, they search grumbling for a new spot. The Cockerel suggests good sites but is ignored. When I open the French windows, the two Buff Orpingtons come in and sit at our feet, like a pair of fluffy slippers.

As I break through the festoons of spiders' webs on my way to the swimming pool, I spot the odd bright jewel of an early tomato, a luscious red plum San Marzano, a golden Jaune St Vincent or a stripy Tigerella that ripens before the main crop, some in pots and some planted in open ground - only a few tomatoes, not enough for a whole salad but just right for breakfast as a juicy topping for my tapenade on wholemeal toast decorated with basil leaves.

To make this quick olive tapenade: rinse a couple of anchovies and a tablespoon of capers and pop them into the blender with a clove of garlic, a sprig of fresh thyme, a spoonful of mustard and two tins of pitted olives. All these good things are mixed with olive oil and lemon juice and can be stored in the fridge for some time sealed with more oil. We have a small olive tree in a large pot that we lovingly ferry from terrace to sunroom season after season.

Pretty frothy yellow flowers sometimes turn to olives but none ever ripen.

Each year I try a selection of tomatoes from Colin Simpson's delightful catalogue and hope it encourages him to invent more good new varieties like the excellent 'John Hawkins' (named after his local pub landlord). I experiment growing tomatoes of every shape, hue and flavour. Almost any sort of tomato can be matched with a basil variety. Suffolk Herbs offer a good range. My favourite at the moment is the tiny leaved Greek basil, it doesn't flop and carries on well into the season, ending up in a pesto of pine nuts, garlic, pecorino and olive oil to pungently flavour soups and pasta dishes.

CTOBER - Walnuts

The pumpkins I planted on the compost heap have grown into a jungle of leaves and tendrils. One branch has raced along the picket fence, and nestling behind the paling is an enormous bright crimson Rouge Vif d'Etampes which we will eat sliced and grilled with cheese - a comforting thought as the lovely blue Crown Prince pumpkins I sowed didn't fruit at all.

Everything must be gathered in before the first frosts. The pretty chillis, peppers and aubergines (var: Slim Jim is particularly nice) that have been enjoying the late summer on the terrace are now ready to eat. The walnuts must be picked up every morning before the squirrels bury them in the garden.

I love my walnut tree and like to eat the nuts now before they dry out. I'm especially fond of these chewy biscuits. **Beat three egg whites till stiff and fold in 3oz chopped walnuts, 3oz light muscovado sugar and 1 oz plain flour. Spoon the mixture on to an oiled baking sheet and bake for 20 minutes till firm. Cool on a rack and keep in a tin.**

Barbara has three walnut trees and makes a delicious relish of apples, dates, onions, mace and nuts. If you run out of pine nuts, walnuts make a good substitute. Wonderful with warm potatoes, hard boiled eggs and red peppers dressed with a vinaigrette of walnut oil and cider vinegar, they are best of all partnered with a glass of red wine and some salty cheese in an Autumn salad.

I can still muster a small bowl of coriander, parsley, salad burnet, rocket, radicchio, purslane, corn salad and perennial garlic chives, all quite strong flavours, which will need a few unfrosted Chinese leaves to calm them down.

The Californian food writer Anna Thomas describes a mouth watering seasonal dish of radicchio, landcress, thinly sliced peppers, Roquefort cheese and walnut pieces served with slices of crisp pear.

OVEMBER - Sweet Potatoes

Anna Thomas' recipes are so good they have made me break my promise to only use homegrown ingredients in these dishes. I can't pretend to grow Sweet Potatoes, although I would love to. As a perennial member of the morning glory family, it has decoratively shaped leaves, gorgeous pink flowers and a wandering habit. According to Joy Larcom there are varieties that grow in southern Europe, but sadly not here.

So I'm cheating, but this version of her vibrantly colourful homely soup fills the kitchen with warmth and replenishes body and soul. **Simmer 1lb of peeled, diced sweet potato with a bayleaf in a heavy casserole dish with a pint of stock till soft. At the same time caramelize a couple of onions in butter in a frying pan. Add the onion to the soup and deglaze the pan juices with the potato stock. Blend till smooth. Pour the mixture back into the heavy pan with 1lb sweetcorn kernels, a diced red pepper and a finely chopped, de-seeded green chilli. Simmer till tender. Serve with a spoonful of crème fraîche and a sprinkle of chopped coriander.** I suppose it could be made with parsnips......

I serve this soup to intrepid customers who brave the autumn gales with a piece of Barbara's Mediterranean Bread. This is actually a basic scone recipe that substitutes olive oil for fat. **Mix together 6oz self-raising flour, 2 tablespoons each of oil and milk, a teaspoon of baking powder and a large egg. Flavour with** mustard powder and cayenne, chopped sundried tomatoes, pickled walnuts or olives and top with fresh rosemary and a little strong cheese - fetta, mature cheddar or parmesan. Homemade bread turns a soup into a meal, and is lovely with this terrine.

In the sunroom, the few last peppers and aubergines linger. A vegetable terrine is a nice souvenir of the year's harvest. I slice and grill the vegetables and at the same time fry some red onions, garlic, courgettes and tomatoes in olive oil till reduced in a pan. The aubergine rounds are then used to line a buttered dish and the purée is added; then a layer of feta or mozzarella cheese, a layer of skinned peppers and finally a topping of parmesan and basil. Cover with foil and place in a medium oven till cooked through. Turn out and leave to cool.

ECEMBER - Quinces

My quince (var: Champion) with its silvery leaves and white flowers is the prettiest tree in the garden. I want to plant other varieties: Meech's Prolific with pear shaped fruit, and Portugal with almost orange quinces. I'll have no difficulty using the surplus fruit and when I fill my beautiful blue bowl with these fragrant golden apples I know that Christmas is here. I've always thought quinces would have been a more convincing temptation for Eve in the garden of Eden.

I put chopped quinces in the Christmas cake, with pecans, pineapple, grated coconut and candied ginger, and in our mincepie filling. I use them instead of, and to enhance the flavour of apples and pears. French children go to school with quince paste (*contignac*) in their lunch boxes. Mine turn up their noses at such sophisticated fare, and it's quite a palaver to make, but is delicious, and elegantly wrapped makes a wonderful Christmas present.

Always wipe any grey fluff off quinces before cooking, and then bake them whole in a medium oven until soft. Cool, core, skin and then cook with a few peeled oranges till sloppy. Sieve, weigh and add an equal amount of sugar to purée. Put the mixture back in the pan, and ignoring the splutters, stir for about half an hour till thick. Place on a flat tray dusted with caster sugar, and leave to dry for several days in a warm place (the airing cupboard, or over

the Rayburn). Cut into small pieces and dredge with icing sugar that has been spiced with powdered cinnamon and ginger.

Finally, here is a recipe for quince ratafia. **Peel, core and grate some yellow quinces. This is a beastly job (your food processor may cope with it) but it's well worth it. Place in a bottle so the final ratio is 1/3 quince to 1/3 spiced sugar and top up with vodka. Leave for a couple of months.**

The year closes in a finale of wind and rain. I tuck the hens in their smart new henhouse and settle down in front of the fire with a pile of seed catalogues to dream of delicacies I will grow in the kitchen garden next year. I'll drink a toast to the old year with a glass of ratafia. Santé.

Favourite Gardening and Cookery Books:

From Anna's Kitchen	Anna Thomas - Penguin
Real Good Food	Nigel Slater - Fourth Estate
Good Things	Jane Grigson - Penguin
A Table in Provence	Leslie Forbes - Penguin
Creative Vegetable Gardening	Joy Larkom - Mitchell Beazley
Building a Wood-Fired Oven	Tom Jaine- Prospect Books

Best Seed Catalogues:

Suffolk Herbs	01376 572 456
Simpson's Seeds	01883 715242
Marshalls	01945 583 407
Nutwood Nurseries	01782 750913
Scotts	01460 72306

Hens, Henhouses and Equipment:

The Henhouse	01379 678664
The Domestic Fowl Trust	01386 833 083

The Kitchen Garden at Troston, Bury St Edmunds, Suffolk sells perennial and vegetable plants, produce, useful hen and garden paraphenalia and is open Fridays and Saturdays from May till October.

Please phone to make sure.   01359 268 322